All Abou
Teeth

written by Jessica Holden

Your Teeth

Your teeth help you.
They help you to eat your food
and they help you to talk.

Not all teeth look the same.
You have sharp teeth called *incisors*.
These help you to cut up your food.

You also have teeth with flat tops.
These are called *molars*.
They help you to *chew* your food.

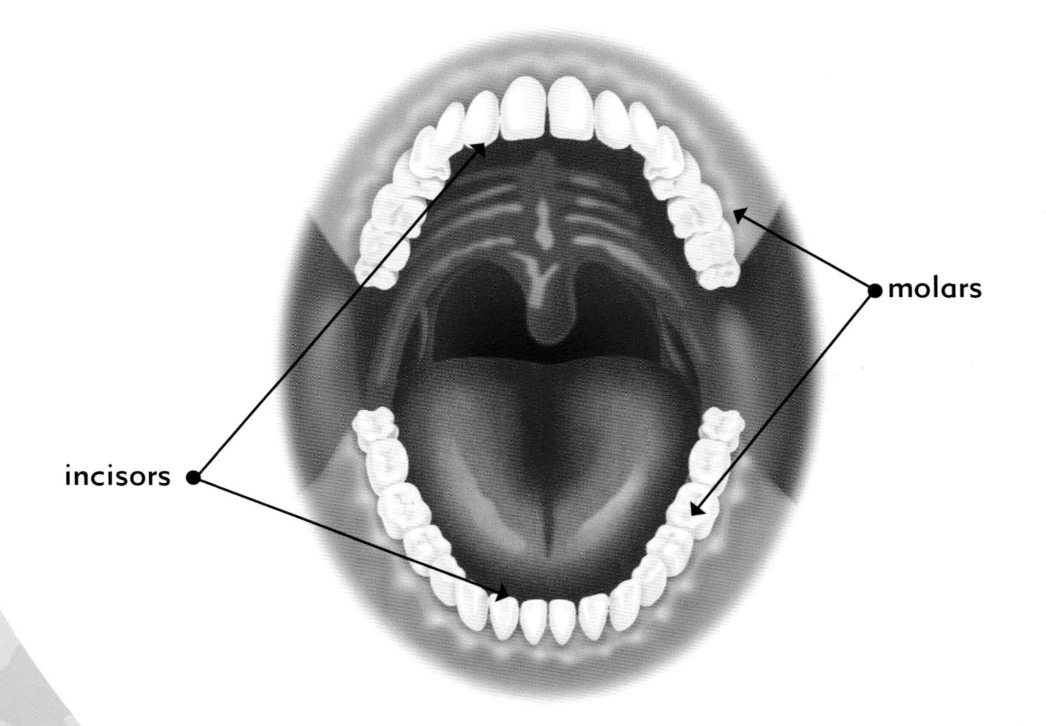

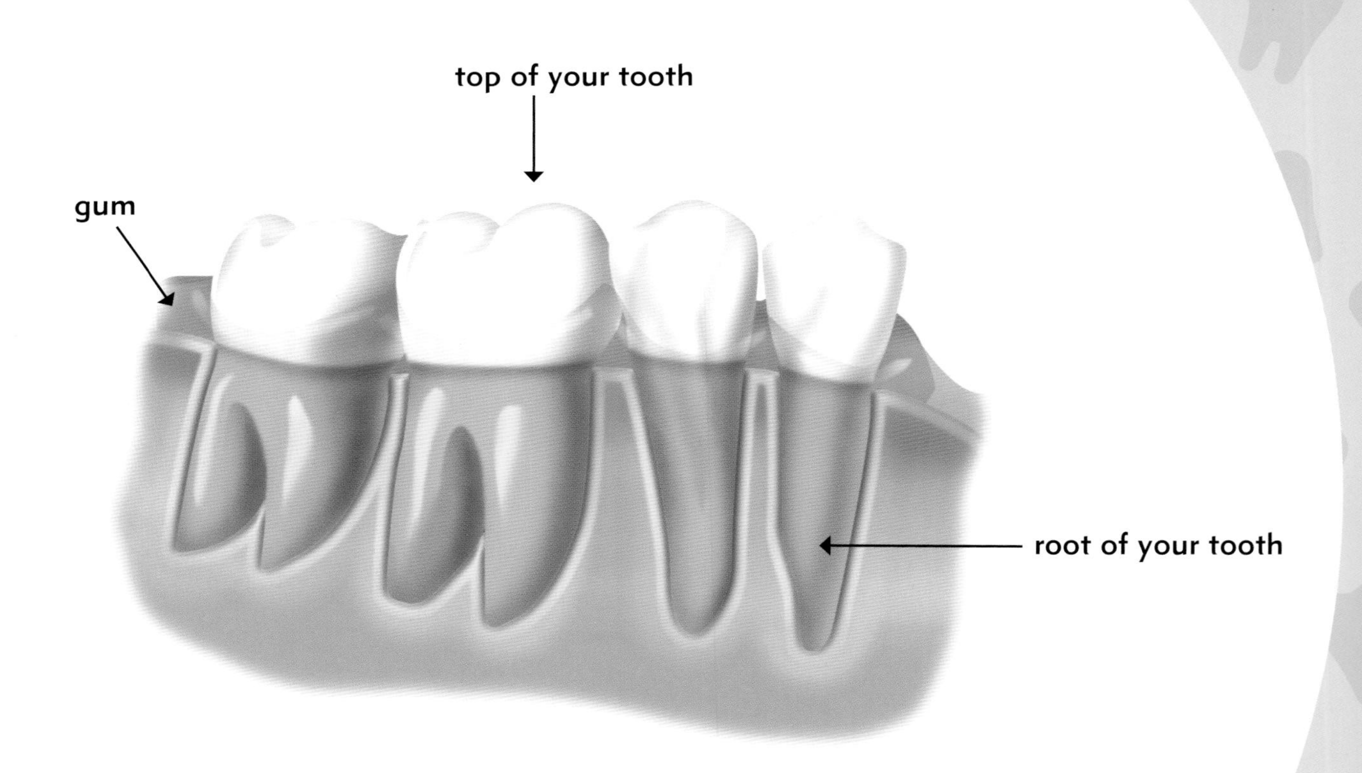

You can only see part of your teeth. Under your *gum*, a tooth has a long *root* to keep it in place.

The outside of your tooth is very hard.
It is the hardest part of your body.
It is called *enamel*.
The inside of your tooth is soft.
This is called *pulp*.

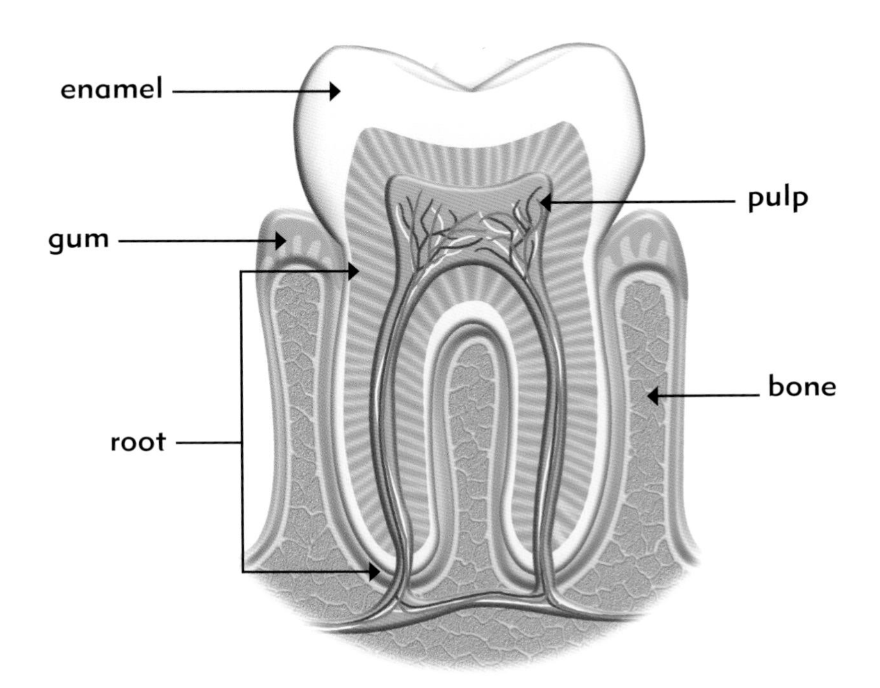

How Many Teeth?

When you were a tiny baby, your teeth were growing under your gums.
When you were a bit older, these teeth started to come out of your gums.

We call these first teeth “baby teeth”.
When you were about three years old,
you had 20 baby teeth.
There were ten at the top and ten at the bottom.

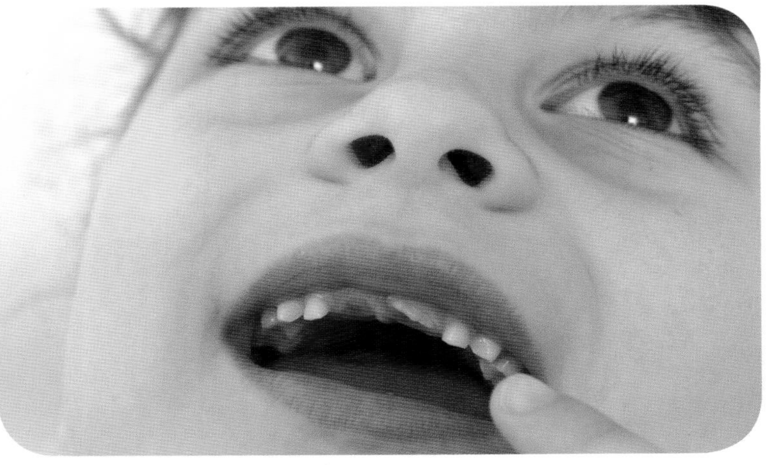

Under your baby teeth there are more teeth growing.
These are called your second teeth.

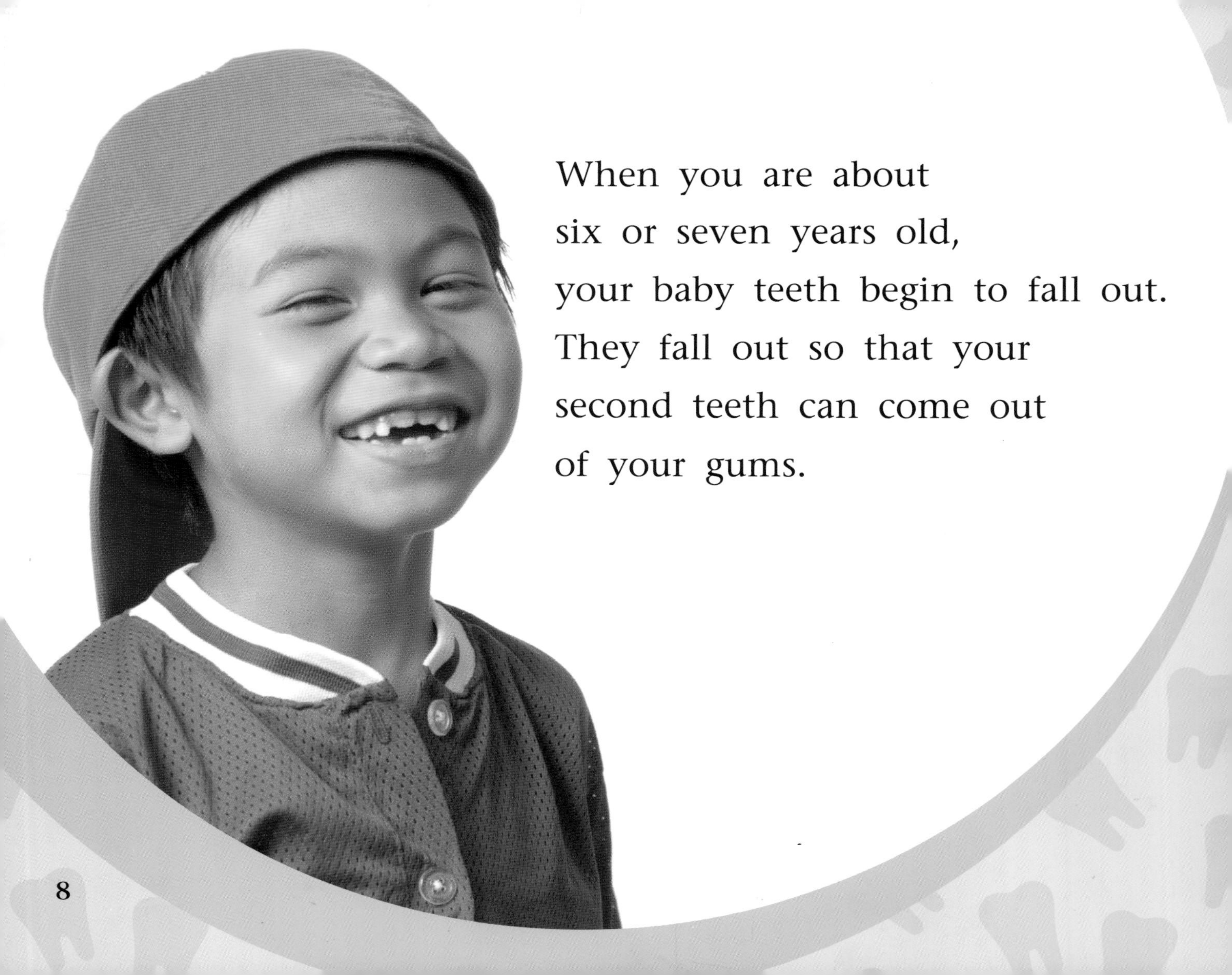

When you are about
six or seven years old,
your baby teeth begin to fall out.
They fall out so that your
second teeth can come out
of your gums.

When you are about 20 years old
you will have all your second teeth.
You will have 32 teeth.

Looking After Your Teeth

There are **four** ways to look after your teeth, so you always have a lovely smile.

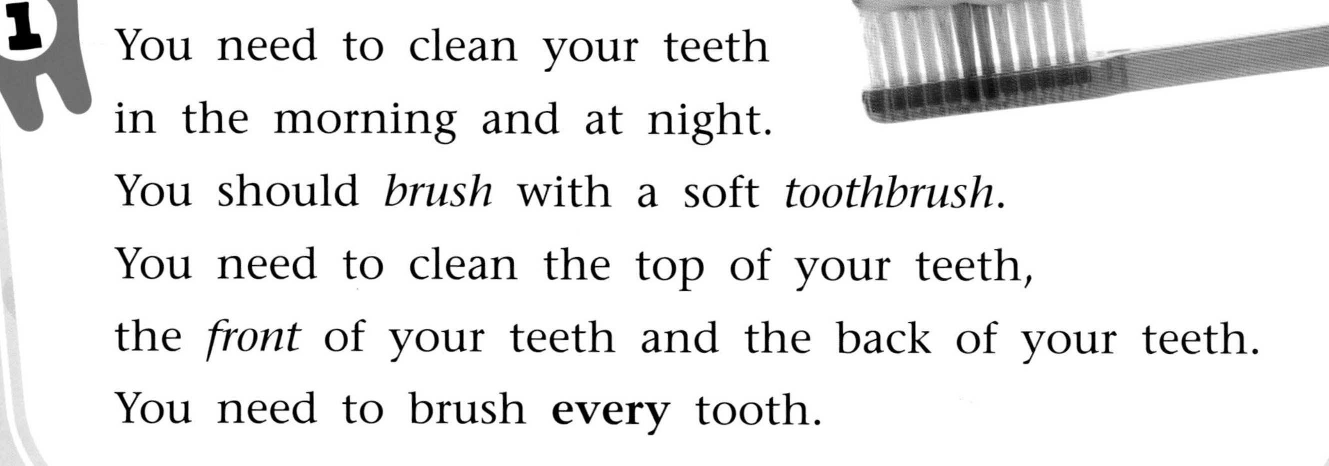

1

You need to clean your teeth in the morning and at night. You should *brush* with a soft *toothbrush*. You need to clean the top of your teeth, the *front* of your teeth and the back of your teeth. You need to brush **every** tooth.

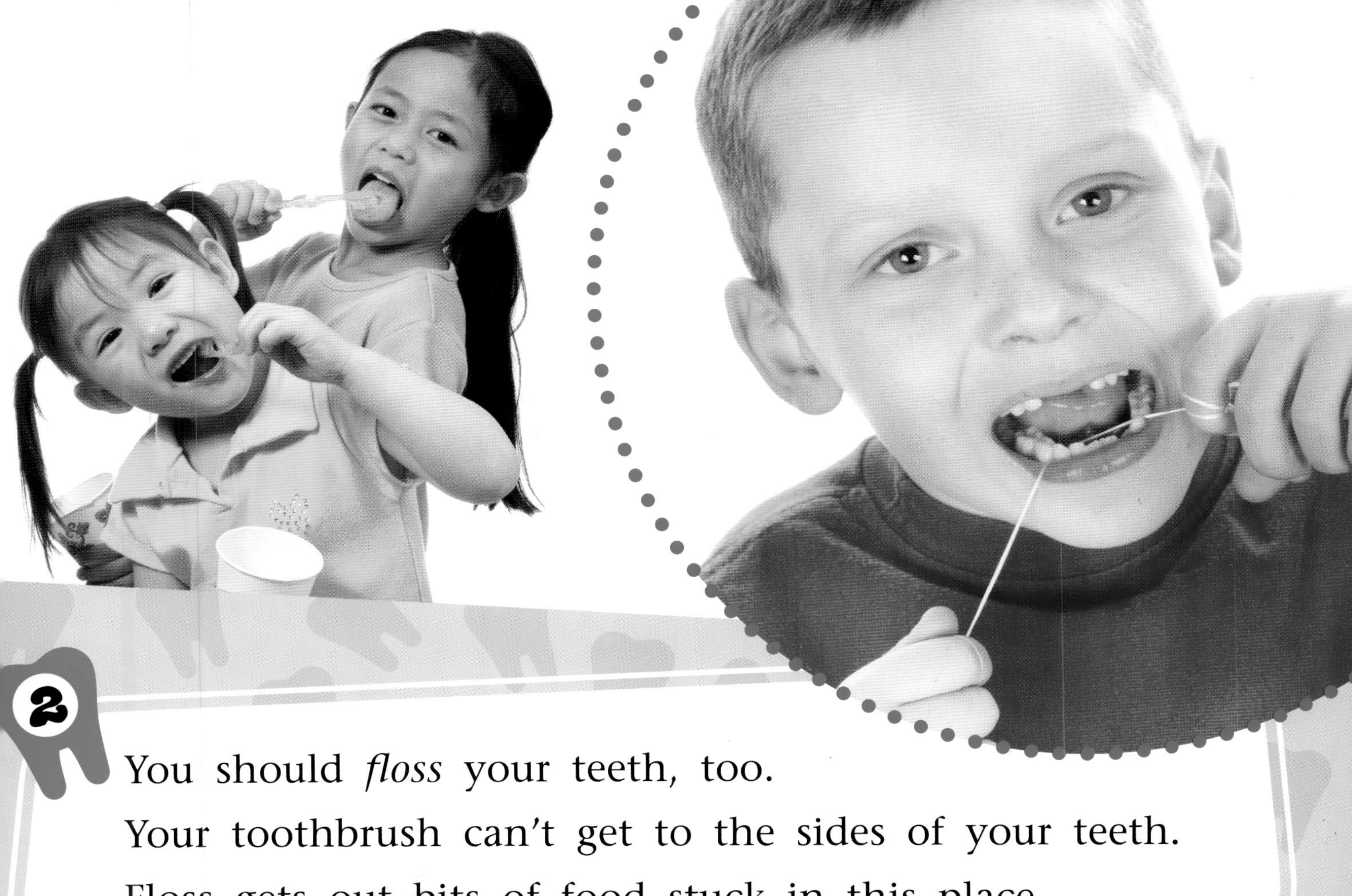

2

You should *floss* your teeth, too.
Your toothbrush can't get to the sides of your teeth.
Floss gets out bits of food stuck in this place.

3

You need to eat good food
to make your teeth strong.
You should not eat or drink too much *sugar*.
Too much sugar makes *holes* in your teeth.

4

You need to see your dentist twice a year. Your dentist will look at your teeth to see if you are taking good care of them.

You need to look after your teeth.
You will have them for a long time!

Picture Glossary

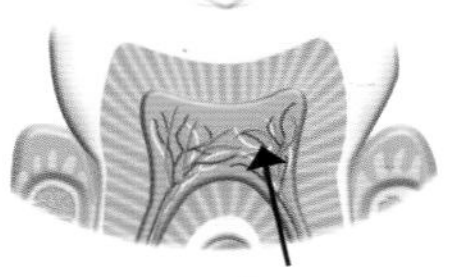
pulp

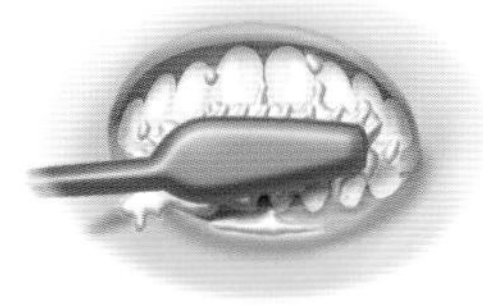
brush

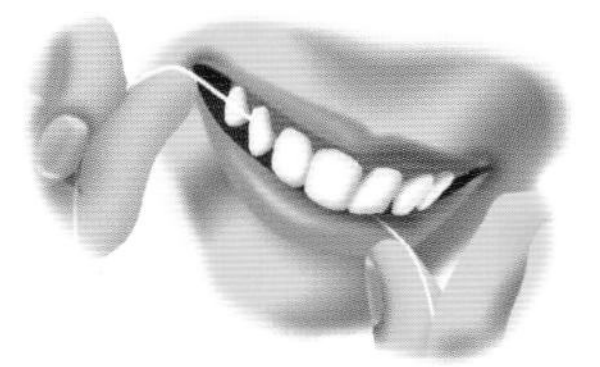
floss

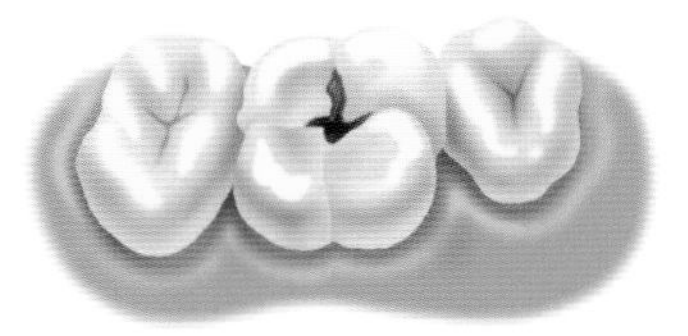
holes

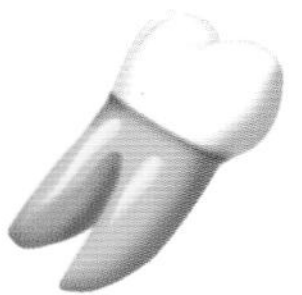
root

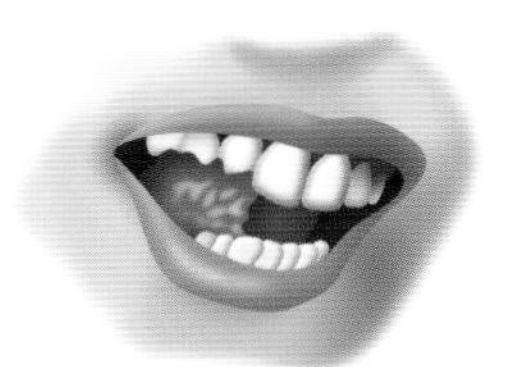
chew

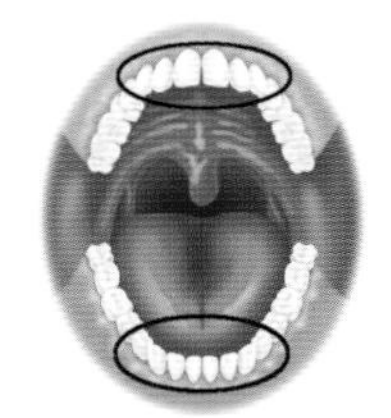
front

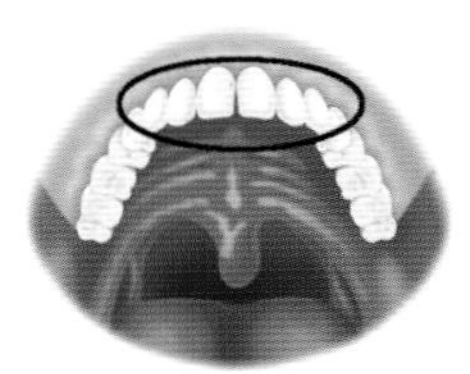
incisors

sugar

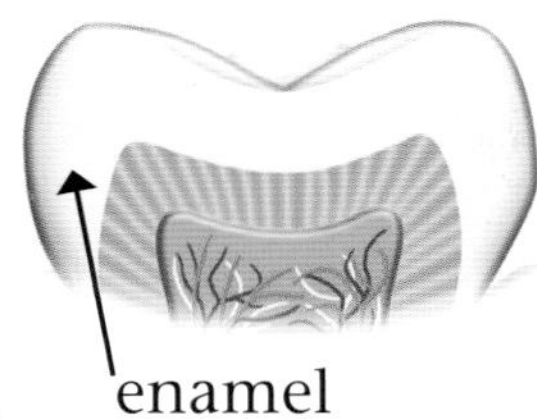
enamel

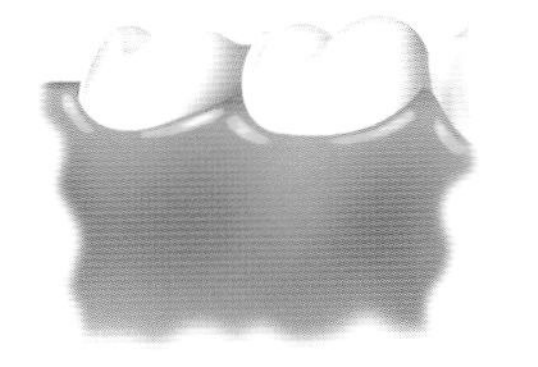
gum

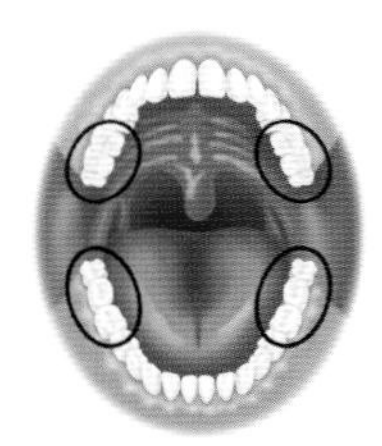
molars

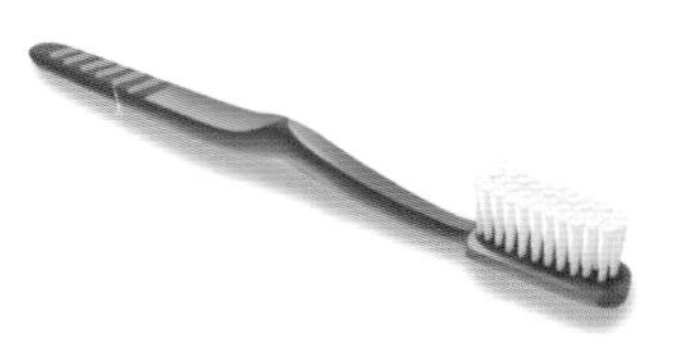
toothbrush